Rad
Cocktails

Rad
Cocktails

by Amanda Greenbaum

CERTIFIED MIXOLOGIST AND CERTIFIED SOMMELIER

Charleston, SC
www.PalmettoPublishing.com

Rad Cocktails

Hardcover ISBN: 978-1-64990-444-7

This book is for all of the suckers who paid twenty dollars for a cocktail last night you could've made at home. It's okay, we've all been there.

Table of Contents

The Bar Necessities

When you're putting together an "at home" bar, no one expects you to have the same materials and ingredients as big restaurants or cocktail bars. But you will need some things.

We're all lazy, so I'll make it as simple as possible.

The following is a cheat sheet of ingredients that will be just enough for pretty much anything that comes your way when hosting or making cocktails at home. You can pick these up at your local supermarket, Target, Walmart, Total Wine, or BevMo! You can probably even order some of it on Amazon. This list is by no means exhaustive. There are plenty of other great liqueurs and spirits I use in my cocktails that you, too, can purchase. But if you want to hit the most check marks while spending the least, this is your list.

The Bar Ingredients

- **THE *FIVE* MAIN SPIRITS:**

  - Vodka
  - Gin
  - Tequila
  - Whiskey
  - Rum
  - (Optional: Scotch and Brandy)

- **THE LIQUEURS/CORDIALS**

  - Triple Sec   orange flavor
  - Blue Curaçao   orange flavor
  - Kahlúa   coffee flavor
  - Baileys   chocolate flavor
  - Amaretto   cherry/almond flavor
  - Campari   bitter orange flavor
  - Aperol   (less) bitter orange flavor
  - Angostura Bitters   cinnamon and herbal flavor
  - Maraschino   cherry flavor

- **OPTIONAL LIQUEURS (used in several of my Original Cocktails)**

St-Germain Elderflower Liqueur	elderflower and lemon flavor
Rose/Geranium Liqueur	rose and geranium flavor
Lychee Liqueur	lychee flavor
Grand Marnier	orange cognac–based liqueur
Cointreau	orange cognac–based liqueur

- **THE CITRUS**

  - Lemons
  - Limes
  - Oranges

- **THE MIXERS**

  - Orange Juice
  - Cranberry Juice
  - Pineapple Juice
  - Grapefruit Juice
  - Club Soda/Soda Water
  - Tonic Water
  - Ginger Beer
  - Coca-Cola
  - Sprite
  - Grenadine
  - Maraschino Cherries
  - Syrups (see Syrup Recipes)

- **GARNISHES**

  - Maraschino or Luxardo Cherries
  - Olives
  - Edible flowers
  - Candies
  - Salt
  - Tajin
  - Citrus Fruits (listed above, including grapefruit)
  - Berries
  - Mint
  - Cucumbers
  - Basil

- **WINE**

  - A Sparkling
    - » Prosecco, Champagne, Sparkling Wine
  - A Crisp White
    - » Sauvignon Blanc, Dry Riesling, Pinot Grigio
  - A Heavier White
    - » Chardonnay, Viognier, White Bordeaux
  - A Rosé
  - A Soft Red
    - » Pinot Noir, Gamay
  - A Heavier Red
    - » Cabernet Sauvignon, Syrah, Merlot

- **BEER**

  - A Lager
  - A Wheat Beer
  - An IPA/Pale Ale

When mixing cocktails, sometimes we're lucky enough that all we need is a glass, a straw, and some ice. But there are a few materials that might come in handy along the way. Let's talk about the important materials and glassware you might need.

The Bar Equipment

Shaker.

There are several types of cocktail shakers out there; the pint glass and tins, shaker/strainer combo, the hawthorn strainer, the julep strainer… They're fancy and have a purpose but nothing you *need* at home. What you need is a simple shaker/strainer combo known as a "cocktail shaker." This is the easiest combo for making cocktails. It provides you with a base to build your cocktails in and a strainer that sits on top of the container when you shake it.

Jigger.

I'm convinced it got its name because bartenders would say, "Hey! Can you pass me that *thingy-ma-jigger*?" when requesting it across the bar. It's that "*thingy-ma-jigger*" we use to measure our pours. Generally, it's great to have two, one that measures a half ounce and an ounce, and another that measures two ounces and one ounce. They're great because they help you measure out accurate pours. Like in baking, proper pour is everything in a cocktail!

Bar spoon.

This isn't your average tablespoon. It's a small spoon with a long stem. This is helpful for mixing cocktails because it's long enough to reach the bottom of several glasses.

Muddler.

This is very important when making drinks that require flavors to be released through mashing fruit, leaves, sugar, and more. It's another helpful mixing agent.

Ice scoop or Tongs.

Self-explanatory.

Fruit juicer.

This is so much easier than squeezing with your hands. Trust me, it's worth the buy!

Corkscrew or wine key.

A very vital tool for opening up wine bottles and even beer bottles too. Generally if you purchase the right corkscrew, a sturdy one (I recommend a double hinge) will last you a while...until you lose it. Not sure why, but I always lose corkscrews!

Toothpicks.

Bar toothpicks are the best. Generally, longer ones are best to use for spearing through garnishes like olives, lemon wheels, or cucumbers.

Straws and stirrers.

Great for decor and for tasting the drinks before serving.

* * *

All right, this is great and all, but what if I don't have those materials yet and I want to make some cocktails?

No problem, there are some great household items you can use in lieu of proper bar tools.

So let's take that list from above and find its household counterparts.

Shaker.

No shaker or strainer? No problem! Let's use a pasta or tea strainer paired with a resealable bottle. The key is to find something you can unseal and reseal tightly and quickly. Hydro Flasks, BlenderBottles, and Mason jars are great alternatives.

Jigger.

Use a tablespoon measurer. 1 tablespoon = 1/2 ounce. You can also use a shot glass, which holds roughly 1.5 ounces.

Bar spoon and muddler.

These go hand in hand. Take your wooden cooking spoon. But here's the ironic twist. For mixing the drink, use the stick end to get maximum length and to mix properly. For muddling, use the top of the spoon for maximum surface area for muddling. Works like a charm.

Ice scoop.

Any plastic cup will do.

Fruit juicer.

You can use your hands, a fork, or a spoon to help get as much juice out as possible.

Corkscrew or wine key. Unfortunately, there is no real way around this one. Just go buy a few. Trust me. The shoe thing doesn't really work.

The Glassware

Yes, the type of glass you use is *actually* important.

Again, we're trying to make this easy, so I won't go into detail about the difference between flutes and tulips and whether you should have a Bordeaux or Burgundy wine glass. Frankly, I'm just happy when my friends have *stemmed* wine glasses.

So for your bar, you'll need the following:

Bucket glasses or highballs. These glasses are your standard cocktail glasses. They are usually the best for multiple-ingredient cocktails like, Sours, Gin and Tonics, and Palomas.

Rocks glasses. These glasses are for spirit-forward cocktails like an Old-Fashioned or a Negroni. Rocks glasses look like bucket glasses but are slightly smaller. You can also use this glass to serve shooters instead of shot glasses.

Martini glasses. These are generally for poured drinks, often from a shaker. They're for the drinks that you don't serve with ice, like Martinis, Lemon Drops, and Manhattans.

Champagne flute. For champagne or sparkling wine. They were created actually for the illusion. The long glass makes the bubbles look endless.

Stemmed wine glass.   I'd recommend ones that are at least thirteen ounces. This is the standard size for a white wine glass, but it will work for red too. A red wine standard pour is five ounces, so this is plenty large.

Shot glasses. These are great for shooters and to use to measure.

Pint glass. This is great for pretty much any beer and also for mixing cocktails.

Optional Glassware

Fiesta Grande. This is the fancy word for margarita glasses. I like them for the appeal. They're not necessary, but they are fun!

Collins glass. This is just a longer, thinner highball used for teas, Tom Collins, and Mojitos.

Coupe glass. This is the original American glass for champagne or sparkling wine, also a fun glass for cocktails with big aromatics. I use these generally for spirit-forward cocktails that don't need ice.

Hurricane glass. This is fun for tiki cocktails: Blue Hawaiian, Zombie, Hurricane, Painkiller, etc.

Brandy snifter. This is great for brandy and whiskey.

Irish coffee mug. This is great for warm drinks like Hot Toddies and Irish coffee.

Cordial glass. This is a small glass for liqueurs and liqueur-based cocktails.

Pilsner glass. This is for lager-style beers.

Belgian beer glass. This is great for wheat and IPA-style beers.

Your bar is stocked, and now you're ready. Let's play ball...

The Classics

Classic Cocktails

Because what's a cocktail book without the classics?

Cosmopolitan

- 1½ oz. vodka

- ¾ oz. triple sec

- ½ oz. lime juice

- 4 oz. cranberry juice

- 1 lemon or lime

Pour all liquid ingredients into a shaker with ice. Shake vigorously for ten seconds. Strain into a martini glass. You can garnish with a lemon wedge or lime wedge.

Moscow Mule

- 1½ oz. vodka

- ½ oz. lime juice

- ginger beer

- optional: mint sprig

Pour all ingredients directly into a drinking glass with ice. Garnish with lime wedge.

Bloody Mary

- 2 oz. vodka

- ½ oz. lemon juice

- 4 dashes of Cholula Hot Sauce

- 4 dashes of buffalo hot sauce

- 4 dashes of Worcestershire sauce

- 1 celery stalk

- tomato or vegetable tomato juice

- Toppings:

  - shrimp, olives, lemon, bacon, pickles, French fries, hamburgers… okay I'm getting carried away.

Place the celery stalk into a collins glass. Pour in ice. Pour all liquid ingredients into a mixing glass and stir. Pour drink from mixing glass into glass with celery. Garnish with all the toppings you desire.

Margarita

- 1½ oz. tequila

- ¾ oz. Cointreau

- ½ oz. lime juice

- sweet and sour mix

Pour all ingredients directly into a Fiesta Grande or bucket glass with ice. Garnish with lime wedge.

Old-Fashioned

- 2 oz. whiskey

- orange peel

- 2 sugar cubes

- maraschino cherries

- 2 dashes of Angostura bitters

Muddle the cherries, bitters, and sugar cubes together in a mixing glass. Pour in two ounces of whiskey. Stir together with a bar spoon. Pour over ice. Take orange peel and squeeze over glass. Brush the glass with the orange peel and drop it in the glass.

Manhattan

- 2 oz. whiskey

- 1 oz. sweet vermouth

- maraschino cherries

- 2 dashes of Angostura bitters

Pour in the whiskey, vermouth and bitters into a shaker and strainer with ice. At this point you can serve it "Up" in a martini glass, or on the rocks. In a martini glass, strain the mix directly into the glass. Drop one cherry in and serve. In a rocks glass, pour entire drink directly into the glass. Garnish with a cherry on top.

Original Daiquiri

- 2 oz. rum

- ½ oz. lime juice

- 1 oz. simple syrup

Pour all ingredients with ice into a shaker. Shake and strain into a martini glass.

Mojito

- 2 oz. rum

- 1 oz. simple syrup

- 6 mint leaves

- ½ oz. lime juice

- soda water

Muddle mint, simple syrup, and lime juice together in a mixing glass. Pour in rum and ice. Pour all ingredients into a highball glass. Pour over soda water. Garnish with a lime.

Long Island Iced Tea

- ½ oz. gin

- ½ oz. vodka

- ½ oz. whiskey

- ½ oz. triple sec

- sweet and sour mix

- Coca-Cola

- cherry or lemon wedge

Pour all ingredients directly over ice into highball glass. Garnish with a cherry or a lemon wedge.

Negroni

- 1 oz. gin

- 1 oz. sweet vermouth

- 1 oz. Campari

Pour all ingredients together in a rocks glass over ice. Garnish with a lemon twist (optional).

The Rad Recipes

Rad Cocktails

ere's a few originals for you—the real rad cocktails. Impress your friends with these tasty drinks, or enjoy them on your couch, in your PJs, with whatever you're bingeing on currently. (That's my favorite way!)

Vodka

The Talk of the Town

- 2 oz. vodka

- 1 oz. sweet and sour mix*

- 1½ oz. fresh-squeezed grapefruit juice

- Sprite and soda water

Pour vodka, sweet and sour mix, and grapefruit juice into mixing glass. Shake with ice and pour over fresh ice in a highball or wine glass. Garnish with a grapefruit wedge.

Lemon Rose Martini

- 1 oz. Deep Eddy lemon vodka

- ¼ oz. rose/geranium liqueur

- ½ oz. sweet and sour mix

Pour all ingredients into a mixing glass with ice. Shake with and strain into a martini glass. Serve with lemon wedge.

The Berry Bomb

- 2 blackberries

- 2 maraschino cherries

- ¼ oz. Blue Curaçao

- 1 oz. blueberry vodka

- ½ oz. lemon juice

Muddle one blackberry and one maraschino cherry with one-quarter ounce of Blue Curaçao in a mixing glass. Pour in the lemon juice and the vodka with ice. Stir together. Pour into a rocks glass. Garnish with a blackberry and a cherry.

Cherritini

- 1 oz. pomegranate vodka

- ½ oz. amaretto

- ½ oz. maraschino cherry juice

- 1 maraschino cherry

Pour all ingredients together in a shaker with ice. Shake and strain into a martini glass. Garnish with a cherry.

TRADER JOE'S®

LEMON
ELDERFLOWER
SODA

SPARKLING BEVERAGE
FLAVORED WITH LEMON
JUICE & ELDERFLOWER
ESSENCE

NET 8.4 FL OZ
(250mL)

Elderflower Me

- 1 oz. TRU Lemon vodka from Greenbar Distillery

- ½ oz. lime juice

- Trader Joe's Lemon Elderflower Soda

- lime wedge

Pour all ingredients directly into a highball over ice. Garnish with the lime wedge.

Strawberry Refresher

- 6 mint leaves

- 2 basil leaves

- 2 strawberries

- ½ oz. sugar

- 1½ oz. vodka

- club soda

Muddle the mint, basil, and strawberries together with the sugar in a mixing glass. Pour in vodka and ice and stir. Pour into a highball glass. Top with club soda. Garnish with a mint sprig.

Not Your Momma's Milkshake

- 2 oz. vanilla vodka

- 1 oz. maraschino liqueur

- 5 strawberries

- 2 large scoops of Cool Whip

- 1 oz. grenadine

Pour all ingredients into a blender with four to five medium-sized ice cubes. Blend and pour into a highball glass. Garnish with a strawberry.

Find Nemo

- 2 oz. vodka

- ½ oz. lemon juice

- ½ oz. lime juice

- ½ oz. triple sec

- ½ oz. Blue Curaçao

- ginger ale

- fish shaped gummies

Grab a fish bowl. Put ice in the bowl. Place the fish gummies within the ice around the bowl so that they are facing outward in the glass. Pour vodka, lemon juice, lime juice, triple sec, and Blue Curaçao into a mixing glass. Stir together and pour into the fish bowl. Top with ginger ale.

RAD Espresso Cocktail

- 2 oz. vodka

- 1 oz. medium or dark roast coffee

- ¾ oz. Godiva chocolate liqueur

- ½ oz. crème de cacao

- ½ oz. almond milk

- chocolate syrup

- 3 coffee beans

Pour chocolate syrup around the inner rim of the martini glass. Stand the martini glass up and let the chocolate drip. In a cocktail mixing glass, pour vodka, coffee, almond milk, chocolate liqueur, and crème de cacao with ice. Shake vigorously and strain into the martini glass. Garnish with three coffee beans.

Orange Dreamsicle Cocktail

- 1½ oz. vanilla vodka

- 1½ oz. orange juice

- 1 oz. Baileys

- 1 orange peel (optional)

- 1 cinnamon stick

Pour vodka, orange juice, and Baileys with ice. Shake and strain into martini glass. Garnish with an orange peel–wrapped cinnamon stick!

AMASS-querade

- 2 oz. AMASS Botanic Vodka

- ½ oz. Chareau Aloe liqueur

- 1 oz. lychee liqueur

- 1 oz. lemon juice

- 1 oz. simple syrup

Pour all ingredients into a shaker with ice. Shake and strain into a martini glass. Garnish with a lemon twist.

Strawberry Mint Mule

- 2 oz. vodka

- 3 strawberries

- 6 mint leaves

- 1 oz. lime juice

- 4 oz. ginger beer

Muddle strawberries and mint leaves in a mixing glass with lime juice and vodka. Pour into a collins glass with ice. Stir and top with ginger beer. Garnish with a mint sprig.

Hibiscus Spritzer

- 2 oz. vodka

- 1 oz. hibiscus simple syrup

- ½ oz. lemon juice

- 6 oz. diet tonic water

Pour all ingredients together directly into a glass over ice. Stir and serve.

Rum

Caribbean Mistress

- 2 oz. coconut rum

- 1 oz. Grand Marnier

- 1 oz. lychee liqueur

- 1 oz. sweetened lime juice

- 4 oz. orange juice

Pour all ingredients together directly into a highball or bucket glass over ice.

Japanese Cherry Blossom

- 1 oz. silver rum

- ½ oz. lychee liqueur

- splash of grenadine

- ¼ oz. simple syrup

- 4 oz. Sprite

- edible flower

Pour all ingredients together into rocks glass over ice. Garnish with an edible flower.

Monito

- 6 mint leaves

- 2 oz. white rum

- 1 oz. lime juice

- 1 oz. simple syrup

- ¼ oz. Blue Curaçao

- soda water

Muddle mint leaves with simple syrup and lime juice into a highball. Add ice. Pour in rum and Blue Curaçao. Top with soda water and stir. Garnish with mint sprig.

Crazy Monkey

- 2 oz. dark rum

- ½ oz. Crème de Banana

- 1 oz. Kahlúa

Pour all ingredients together in a rocks glass with ice. Stir and serve.

Wine

Simple Sangria

- 4 oz. citron vodka

- fresh fruit, cut up: apples, oranges, berries

- 6 oz. orange juice

- 6 oz. cranberry juice

- 1 bottle of any red wine

- 1½ oz. simple syrup

Soak fruit in the vodka overnight. Pour all ingredients into a large pitcher together with some ice. Stir together until mixed well.

Stupid Good Sangria!

- ½ c. fruity white wine

- ¼ oz. Grand Marnier

- ¼ oz. elderflower liqueur

- ¼ oz. lychee liqueur

- cranberry juice

- orange-flavored sparkling water

- maraschino cherries

Pour wine, Grand Marnier, elderflower liqueur, and lychee liqueur into a pitcher with ice. Add a splash of cranberry juice and orange sparkling water for taste. Garnish with maraschino cherries. Stir and serve.

MOM-mosa

- 1 oz. citron vodka

- ½ oz. peach schnapps

- ½ oz. Cointreau or triple sec

- 1 fresh-cut strawberry

- prosecco

Pour all ingredients into a champagne glass. Top with prosecco.

90+ Spritzer

- ½ oz. lemon juice

- ½ oz. orange liqueur

- ½ oz. elderflower liqueur

- 6 oz. 90-Plus Cellars Prosecco

Pour all ingredients into a wine glass with ice. Slice up extra lemons to put inside the drink as garnish.

Holiday Sangria

Makes two pitchers.

- 1 bottle of red wine

- ice

- 2 c. brandy

- ½ c. Cointreau

- ¼ tsp. ground cloves

- ½ tsp. cinnamon

- 2 tsp. brown sugar

- 1 c. orange juice

- 1 c. cranberry juice

- sliced apples, sliced oranges, and cranberries

- 4 big cinnamon sticks

In a bowl, soak the fruit and cinnamon sticks in brandy. Let it sit overnight. The next morning, pour all of the ingredients in together and mix. Add more cranberry juice and orange juice to taste.

Tequila

Strawberry Margarita

Makes two.

- 3 fresh strawberries

- 3 frozen strawberries

- ½ c. tequila

- ¼ c. triple sec

- ½ c. lime juice

- ½ c. simple syrup

- ¼ c. lemon juice

Pour all ingredients into a blender. Add in the ice—liquid should meet ice halfway up the ice for best texture. Blend and pour into margarita glasses. Garnish with a lime.

* Want salt? Rim the glass with a used lime. Pour margarita salt onto a plate and dip the margarita rim into the salt plate. Then pour in the drink.

Blue Margarita

- 1 oz. Reposado tequila

- ½ oz. lemon juice

- 1½ oz. lime juice

- ½ oz. simple syrup

- ½ oz. Blue Curaçao

- 1 egg white

- 1 edible flower

Pour the tequila, the Blue Curaçao, and the sweet and sour mix into a shaker tin. Shake all ingredients and strain into glass.

Then shake separately the egg white until frothy. Pour over glass and add a flower garnish.

Blood Orange Paloma

- 1½ oz. silver tequila

- ½ oz. fresh-squeezed lime juice

- 6 oz. blood orange soda

- 1 orange

- 1 lime

Pour directly into a glass with ice, tequila, lime juice, and blood orange soda. Stir with a mixing spoon and garnish with an orange and a lime wedge.

La Gringa

- 2 oz. tequila

- 3 blackberries

- ¾ oz. Cointreau

- ½ oz. lemon juice

- ½ oz. lime juice

- 3 oz. lemonade

- 3 oz. guava juice

Muddle blackberries into a mixing glass. Pour in Cointreau, lemon juice, lime juice, lemonade, guava juice, and tequila. Add ice and stir. Pour into a highball, Mason jar, or any larger glass.

Sugar-Free Tangy Marg

- 2 oz. tequila blanco

- 1 oz. lime juice

- ½ oz. lemon juice

- 1 oz. stevia simple syrup

- 3 dashes of Tajin

- Tajin rim and lime wedge for garnish

Pour tequila, lime juice, lemon juice, simple syrup, and Tajin into a shaker. Rim the glass by using lime juice and then pouring Tajin on top. Shake with ice and strain into a glass with new ice. Garnish with a lime wedge.

Passion Fruit Sunrise Margarita

- 2 oz. silver tequila

- 1½ oz. lime juice

- ½ oz. lemon juice

- 1 oz. passion fruit syrup

- ¾ oz. Fair Drinks kumquat liqueur

- ¼ oz. grenadine

- 2 dashes of Trader Joe's chili lime seasoning or Tajin

- ½ lime

Pour all ingredients into a shaker with ice. Shake vigorously. Rim the rocks glass with lime juice and chili lime seasoning. Add ice to glass and pour the drink over. Garnish with a lime wheel.

Raspberry Blended Margarita

Makes two.

- 5 oz. Reposado tequila

- 1 scoop frozen raspberries

- 4–5 fresh raspberries

- 3 limes, squeezed

- 2 lemons, squeezed

- 2 oz. simple syrup

- 1½ oz. Cointreau

Pour all ingredients into a blender. Add in the ice—liquid should meet ice three-quarters of the way up the ice for best texture. Blend and pour into margarita glasses.

* Want salt? Rim the glass with a used lime. Pour margarita salt onto a plate and dip the margarita rim into the salt plate. Then pour in the drink.

Apple Marg

- 2 oz. tequila

- ½ oz. triple sec

- 1½ lime

- 1 oz. sour apple mix

Pour all ingredients into a blender. Add in the ice—liquid should meet ice halfway up the ice for best texture. Blend and pour into margarita glasses. Garnish with a lime.

* Want salt? Rim the glass with a used lime. Pour margarita salt onto a plate and dip the margarita rim into the salt plate. Then pour in the drink.

Gin

SOMMthing
Rad Gin 42

- 1½ oz. Hendricks gin

- 1 oz. simple syrup

- ½ lemon, squeezed

- ginger beer

- lemon for garnish

Pour straight into champagne flute over ice, gin, simple syrup, and lemon juice. Mix together and then top with ginger beer. Garnish with a lemon wedge.

AMASS

DRY GIN
LOS ANGELES

GRAPEFRUIT · CALIFORNIA BAY LEAF · CARDAMOM

Juniper, Coriander, Cedar Berry and Bark, Rosemary,
Angelica, Orris, Cassia, Fennel, Licorice, Cubeb,
Cascara Sagrada, Cacao, Cardamom, California Bay
Leaf, Ginger, Fresh Lemon Peel, Fresh Grapefruit Peel,
Bitter Orange Peel, Dried Lemon Peel, Hibiscus, Lion's
Mane Mushroom, Reishi Mushroom, Clove, Nutmeg,
Ashwagandha, Sarsaparilla, Long Pepper, Grains of
Paradise, Kaffir Lime Leaf

45% ALC/VOL
90 PROOF
750ML

DISTILLED AND BOTTLED
IN DOWNTOWN L.A.

15mg C

REA

citrus blend

Citrus Twist

- 2 oz. gin

- 1 oz. Cointreau orange liqueur

- 1 oz. Real Drinks citrus blend

- 1 oz. fresh lemon juice

- 1 lemon, squeezed

Pour all ingredients into a shaker. Shake over ice and strain into a martini glass. Garnish with a lemon wedge or twist.

This Sh*t's Gonna Kick Your A$$

- 1 oz. gin

- 1 oz. coffee liqueur

- 1 oz. triple sec

- ¼ oz. Kahlúa

- 1 egg white

- Angostura House bitters

Pour all ingredients into a shaker. Shake well and strain into a coupe glass. Garnish with bitters.

Simple Mint Martini

- 2 oz. gin

- 1 oz. simple syrup

- ½ lime, squeezed

- 8 Apple mint leaves

Pour all ingredients into a shaker over ice. Shake and double-strain into a martini glass.

Anti-British British Cocktail

- 2 oz. Empress 1908 gin

- ½ oz. lemon juice

- 1 oz. Chareau Aloe liqueur

- ¾ oz. St-Germain elderflower liqueur

- ¾ oz. Blue Curaçao

- diet tonic water

- maraschino cherries

Pour the gin, lemon juice, Chareau, and elderflower liqueur into a shaker. Add ice and shake. Pour into a bucket or highball glass over ice. Top with diet tonic water and garnish with cherries.

LA Lemonade

- 1 oz. gin

- ½ oz. triple sec

- soda water

- sweet and sour mix

- lemon wheel for garnish

Pour straight into glass gin, triple sec, soda water, and sweet and sour mix over ice. Garnish with a lemon wheel.

AMASS Lemonade

- 2 oz. AMASS Los Angeles Dry Gin

- 1 oz. St-Germain elderflower liqueur

- 1 oz. simple syrup

- 1 oz. lemon juice

Pour the gin, elderflower liqueur, simple syrup, and lemon juice into a shaker. Shake on ice and pour into rocks glass. Garnish with lemon twist.

CBD's Knees

- 1½ oz. AMASS gin

- ½ oz. Disaronno amaretto

- ½ oz. passion fruit syrup

- 1/10 lemon, squeezed

- 1/10 egg white

- 1/10 10-mg stick of One Love Tea CBD-infused honey

Pour into a shaker the gin, amaretto, passion fruit syrup, lemon, and egg white. Take half of the honey stick and pour into the mix. Shake with ice and pour with ice into rimmed glass. Garnish with the other half of the honey stick around the rim of the glass and a lemon wedge.

#Rosebud

- 1½ oz. gin

- 1 oz. St-Germain elderflower liqueur

- ½ oz. lemon juice

- Fentimans Rose Lemonade

- cane sugar

- 1 lemon, squeezed

Mix together gin, St-Germain, and lemon juice in a mixing glass. Top with Fentimans Rose Lemonade. Garnish with sugar rim and lemon.

Cherry Bomb

- 2 oz. Hendricks Gin

- 1 oz. maraschino cherry liqueur

- 1 oz. grenadine

- ½ oz. Disaronno amaretto

- ½ oz. lime juice

- ginger beer

- maraschino cherries

- 1 lime

Shake gin, maraschino liqueur, grenadine, amaretto, and lime juice in a shaker. Pour over ice into a Collins glass. Top with ginger beer. Mix with a mixing spoon and garnish with a cherry and lime.

Paradise Lost

- 2 oz. Empress gin

- ½ oz. Bols lychee liqueur

- ½ oz. passion fruit syrup

- Sprite or lemon-lime soda

- edible flower for garnish

Pour the gin, lychee liqueur, and passion fruit syrup into a mixing glass with ice. Pour into a bucket or highball glass over ice. Top with Sprite and garnish with an edible flower.

Whiskey (SWEET and) Sour

- 1½ oz. whiskey

- 3 oz. sweet and sour mix

- 1 oz. Coca-Cola regular

- 1 egg white

- Angostura bitters

Combine whiskey and sweet and sour mix with egg white. Dry shake the ingredients in the shaker for ten seconds. Then add ice and shake vigorously for ten more seconds or until frothy. Pour the components of the shaker into glass. Then, pour Coca-Cola on top of ice in a glass. Top it off with a few dashes of Angostura bitters.

Boozy Latte

- 2 oz. espresso

- 1 oz. Skrewball peanut butter whiskey

- 4 oz. frothy almond milk

- sugar for taste (how do you take your coffee?)

- espresso beans

Froth the almond milk. If you don't have a frother at home, shake 4 oz. of almond milk in a jar for thirty seconds, then microwave it for thirty. Repeat until frothy.

When your milk is frothed, combine espresso, whiskey, sugar, and almond milk in a shaker. Shake together for five seconds lightly. Pour into an espresso cup and garnish with espresso beans on top.

Caramel
Milkshaketini

- 1½ oz. whiskey

- 1 oz. L'Orgeat liqueur

- ½ oz. simple syrup

- 1 egg white

Combine all ingredients into a shaker. Shake vigorously with ice for twenty seconds. Strain into a martini glass.

PBWHSKY

- 2 oz. Skrewball peanut butter whiskey

- 1 oz. coffee flavor liqueur

- 2 tbsp. vanilla ice cream

- 1 oz. L'Orgeat liqueur

- cinnamon

Combine all ingredients in a shaker. Shake vigorously for ten seconds. Open and add ice. Close and shake again for five seconds. Pour in a martini glass and garnish with a dash of cinnamon.

Tennessee Paloma

- 1½ oz. Jack Daniel's whiskey

- ½ oz. simple syrup

- 2 oz. grapefruit juice

- club soda

Add the whiskey, simple syrup, and grapefruit juice to a shaker. Shake vigorously with ice for five seconds. Set aside. Use a rocks glass and fill with crushed ice. Pour the drink over the crushed ice. Top with club soda.

Washington Apple Crisp

- 1 oz. Crown Royal whiskey

- 1 oz. Sour Apple Pucker Schnapps

- ¾ oz. cranberry juice

- 4 oz. Angry Orchard crisp apple cider

Pour and mix together the whiskey, schnapps, cranberry juice, and hard cider over ice. Enjoy.

Frisky Sour Smash

- 2 oz. bourbon

- 1 lime

- ½ lemon, squeezed

- 1 clementine

- 1 tbsp. cane sugar

- 1 lime, squeezed

Juice the fruits and stir in the sugar and whiskey. Pour over ice and garnish with a lime.

Whiskey on the (La)Roccas

- 2 oz. whiskey

- 1 oz. fresh-squeezed orange juice

- 2 sugar cubes

- ginger beer

- orange slice

Muddle the sugar cubes in a mixing glass. Stir the whiskey, orange juice, and sugar. Strain and pour into a rocks glass over ice. Top with ginger beer. Garnish with an orange slice.

Spiked Mo' Joe

- 2 oz. bourbon

- 1 oz. Kahlúa

- 4 oz. almond milk

- dash of cinnamon

Shake all ingredients together on ice and pour over ice! Garnish with cinnamon and enjoy!

Waiting For You

- 2 oz. bourbon or rye whiskey

- 1 oz. crème de cassis

- ¼ oz. simple syrup

- lemon peel for garnish

Combine rye whiskey, crème de cassis, and simple syrup together in a shaker. Shake on ice and pour over ice! Garnish with a lemon peel.

Friskey Whiskey

- 2 oz. bourbon

- ¾ oz. Cointreau

- 1 egg white, shaken

- 1 oz. Friskey simple syrup

- orange peel

Remove the egg white from the yolk and discard the yolk. Pour the egg white into a shaker and close the top. Shake vigorously for fifteen to twenty seconds. Open the top and pour in the bourbon, Cointreau, Friskey syrup, and ice. Shake again vigorously and strain into a martini glass. Garnish with the orange peel.

The Syrups
and Mixers

The Syrups
and Mixers

Nothing is better than making your mixers at home. This is truly the difference between a decent cocktail and a great one! Most bars know this, and top bars use fresh ingredients made from scratch. Seems like a lot of work, I know…we're all lazy! But these take around five minutes each to prepare, and they're great for around four to ten cocktails! Here's how you can make them at home.

Simple Syrup

Makes 10 oz.

- 1 c. water

- 1 c. cane sugar

Mix the water and the cane sugar together in a pot over a high-heat stove. Stir sugar until the granules dissolve completely. Pour into a glassware container and store in a cool space overnight. This should be good for around seven to ten days if kept in the refrigerator.

Stevia Syrup

Makes 10 oz.

- 1 c. water

- 24 mini packets of Stevia sweetener

Mix the water and the sweetener together in a pot over a high-heat stove. Stir until the granules dissolve completely. Pour into a glassware container and store in a cool space overnight. This should be good for around twelve to sixteen days if kept in the refrigerator.

Friskey Simple Syrup

- 1 c. cane sugar

- 1 c. water

- 1 tsp. ginger

- 1 tsp. cloves

- 1 cinnamon stick

- 2 tbsp. mixture of the following spices to taste: star anise, coriander, orange peel, nutmeg

Mix all of the components together over high heat. Put the heat on high and stir until the sugar dissolves. Let it steep for thirty minutes, then strain and pour into a container for storage up to fourteen days.

Sweet and Sour Mixer

If you don't want to make fresh margaritas every time but you want the fresh taste, use this recipe to make margarita mix. All you have to do is add tequila!

- 7 medium lemons

- 12 large limes

- 1½ c. simple syrup (see simple syrup recipe)

- Optional: 1¼ c. Cointreau

Squeeze the lemons and limes into a large container that holds four cups. Add in the simple syrup and the Cointreau. Stir until all of the components are mixed together. Seal and store in a cold area for four to five days.

Honey Syrup

- ½ c. honey

- 1 c. water

Mix honey in one cup of boiling water. Stir until honey is completely dissolved. Store in the refrigerator and use for up to fourteen days.

Now that you've got your bar stocked and your cocktails flowing… Where's my invite?

Always remember to drink responsibly and tastefully. For more up-to-date information, you can follow me on Instagram @SOMMthing.Rad or visit my website: www.sommthingrad.com.

Yeah, that was a shameless plug… I wrote the damn book, so what did you expect?

Recipe Index

W